FALCON

BEAVER

DEER

WOODPECKER

SALMON

BROWN BEAR

THE LITTLE LIBRARY OF
EARTH MEDICINE

WOODPECKER

Kenneth Meadows
Illustrations by Jo Donegan

DK PUBLISHING, INC.

A DK PUBLISHING BOOK

The Little Library of Earth Medicine was
produced, edited, and designed by
GLS Editorial and Design
Garden Studios, 11-15 Betterton Street
London WC2H 9BP

Editorial director: Jane Laing
Design director: Ruth Shane
Project designer: Luke Herriott
Editors: Claire Calman, Terry Burrows, Victoria Sorzano
US Editors: Jennifer Dorr, William Lach, Barbara Minton

Additional illustrations: Roy Flooks 16, 17, 31; John Lawrence 38
Special photography: Mark Hamilton
Picture credits: American Natural History Museum 8-9, 12, 14-15;
San Diego Museum of Man (photograph by John Oldenkamp) 32

First American Edition, 1998
2 4 6 8 10 9 7 5 3 1

Published in the United States by DK Publishing, Inc.
95 Madison Avenue, New York, NY 10016
Visit us on the World Wide Web at http://www.dk.com.

Library of Congress Cataloging-in-Publication Data
Meadows, Kenneth.
    The little library of earth medicine / by Kenneth Meadows. – 1st American ed.
        p.   cm.
    Contents: |1| Falcon, 21st March-19th April – |2| Beaver, 20th April-20 May – |3|
Deer, 21st May-20th June – |4| Woodpecker, 21st June-21st July – |5| Salmon, 22nd July-
21st August – |6| Brown Bear, 22nd August-21st September – |7| Crow, 22nd
September-22nd October – |8| Snake, 23rd October-22nd November – |9| Owl, 23rd
November-21st December – |10| Goose, 22nd December-19 January – |11| Otter, 20th
January-18th February – |12| Wolf, 19th February-20th March.
    Includes indexes.
    ISBN 0-7894-2875-X
    1. Medicine wheels–Miscellanea. 2. Horoscopes. 3. Indians of North
America–Religion–Miscellanea. 4. Typology (Psychology)–Miscellanea. I. Title.
BF1623.M43M42 1998
133.5'9397–dc21
                                                                    97-42267
                                                                    CIP

Reproduced by Kestrel Digital Colour Ltd, Chelmsford, Essex
Printed and bound in Hong Kong by Imago

CONTENTS

INTRODUCING
EARTH MEDICINE

TO NATIVE AMERICANS, MEDICINE IS NOT AN EXTERNAL SUBSTANCE BUT AN INNER POWER THAT IS FOUND IN BOTH NATURE AND OURSELVES.

Earth Medicine is a unique method of personality profiling that draws on Native American understanding of the Universe, and on the principles embodied in sacred Medicine Wheels.

Native Americans believed that spirit, although invisible, permeated Nature, so that everything in Nature was sacred. Animals were perceived as acting as

messengers of spirit. They also appeared in waking dreams to impart power known as "medicine." The recipients of such dreams honored the animal species that appeared to them by rendering their images on ceremonial, ornamental, and everyday artifacts.

NATURE WITHIN SELF
Native American shamans – tribal wisemen – recognized similarities between the natural forces prevalent during the seasons and the characteristics of those born

Shaman's rattle
Shamans used rattles to connect with their inner spirit. This is a Tlingit shaman's wooden rattle.

"Spirit has provided you with an opportunity to study in Nature's university." **Stoney teaching**

during corresponding times of the year. They also noted how personality is affected by the four phases of the Moon – at birth and throughout life – and by the continual alternation of energy flow, from active to passive. This view is encapsulated in Earth Medicine, which helps you to recognize how the dynamics of Nature function within you and how the potential strengths you were born with can be developed.

Animal ornament

To the Anasazi, who carved this ornament from jet, the frog symbolized adaptability.

Wheels, due to their similarity to the spoked wheels of the wagons that carried settlers into the heartlands of once-Native American territory. Each Medicine Wheel showed how different objects or qualities related to one another within the context of a greater whole, and how different forces and energies moved within it.

One Medicine Wheel might be regarded as the master wheel because it indicated balance within Nature and the most effective way of achieving harmony with the Universe and ourselves. It is upon this master Medicine Wheel (see pp.10–11) that Earth Medicine is structured.

MEDICINE WHEELS

Native American cultural traditions embrace a variety of circular symbolic images and objects. These sacred hoops have become known as Medicine

Feast dish

Stylized bear carvings adorn this Tlingit feast dish. To the Native American, the bear symbolizes strength and self-sufficiency.

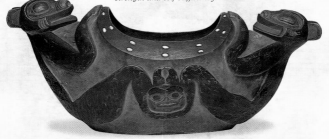

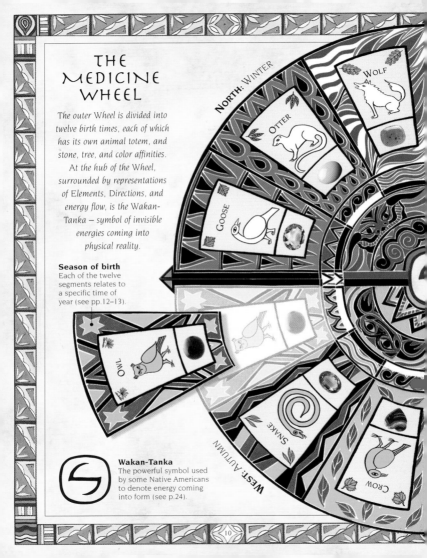

THE MEDICINE WHEEL

The outer Wheel is divided into twelve birth times, each of which has its own animal totem, and stone, tree, and color affinities.

At the hub of the Wheel, surrounded by representations of Elements, Directions, and energy flow, is the Wakan-Tanka – symbol of invisible energies coming into physical reality.

Season of birth
Each of the twelve segments relates to a specific time of year (see pp.12–13).

Wakan-Tanka
The powerful symbol used by some Native Americans to denote energy coming into form (see p.24).

NORTH: WINTER

WEST: AUTUMN

WOLF

OTTER

GOOSE

OWL

SNAKE

CROW

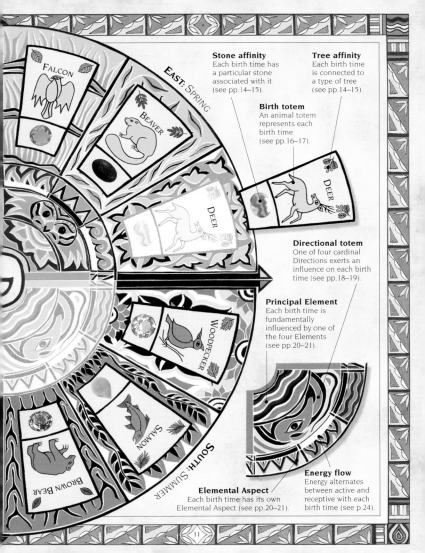

Stone affinity
Each birth time has a particular stone associated with it (see pp.14–15).

Tree affinity
Each birth time is connected to a type of tree (see pp.14–15).

Birth totem
An animal totem represents each birth time (see pp.16–17).

Directional totem
One of four cardinal Directions exerts an influence on each birth time (see pp.18–19).

Principal Element
Each birth time is fundamentally influenced by one of the four Elements (see pp.20–21).

Energy flow
Energy alternates between active and receptive with each birth time (see p.24).

Elemental Aspect
Each birth time has its own Elemental Aspect (see pp.20–21).

EAST: SPRING

SOUTH: SUMMER

FALCON

BEAVER

DEER

DEER

WOODPECKER

SALMON

BROWN BEAR

THE TWELVE
BIRTH TIMES

THE STRUCTURE OF THE MEDICINE WHEEL IS BASED UPON THE SEASONS TO REFLECT THE POWERFUL INFLUENCE OF NATURE ON HUMAN PERSONALITY.

he Medicine Wheel classifies human nature into twelve personality types, each corresponding to the characteristics of Nature at a particular time of the year. It is designed to act as a kind of map to help you discover your strengths and weaknesses, your inner drives and instinctive behaviors, and your true potential.

The four seasons form the basis of the Wheel's structure, with the Summer and Winter solstices and the Spring and Autumn equinoxes marking each season's passing. In Earth Medicine,

each season is a metaphor for a stage of human growth and development. Spring is likened to infancy and the newness of life, and Summer to the exuberance of youth and of rapid development. Autumn represents the fulfillment that mature adulthood brings, while Winter symbolizes the accumulated wisdom that can be drawn upon in later life.

Each seasonal quarter of the Wheel is further divided into three periods, making twelve time segments altogether. The time of your birth determines the direction from which

Seasonal rites

Performers at the Iroquois mid-Winter ceremony wore masks made of braided maize husks. They danced to attune themselves to energies that would ensure a good harvest.

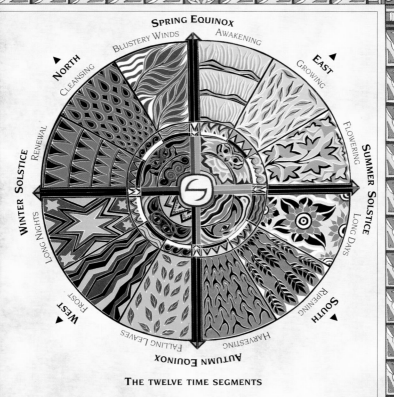

SPRING EQUINOX

BLUSTERY WINDS · AWAKENING

▲ NORTH · EAST ▲

CLEANSING · GROWING

RENEWAL · FLOWERING

WINTER SOLSTICE · SUMMER SOLSTICE

LONG NIGHTS · LONG DAYS

FROST · RIPENING

◀ WEST · SOUTH ▶

FALLING LEAVES · HARVESTING

AUTUMN EQUINOX

THE TWELVE TIME SEGMENTS

you perceive life, and the qualities imbued in Nature in that season are reflected in your core character.

Each of the twelve time segments, or birth times, is named after a feature in the natural yearly cycle. For

example, the period after the Spring equinox is called Awakening time because it is the time of new growth, while the segment after the Autumn equinox is named after the falling leaves that characterize that time.

THE SIGNIFICANCE OF
TOTEMS

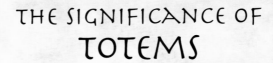

NATIVE AMERICANS BELIEVED THAT TOTEMS — ANIMAL SYMBOLS — REPRESENTED ESSENTIAL TRUTHS AND ACTED AS CONNECTIONS TO NATURAL POWERS.

A totem is an animal or natural object adopted as an emblem to typify certain distinctive qualities. Native Americans regarded animals, whose behavior is predictable, as particularly useful guides to categorizing human patterns of behavior.

A totem mirrors aspects of your nature and unlocks the intuitive knowledge that lies beyond the reasoning capacity of the intellect. It may take the form of a carving or molding, a pictorial image, or a token of fur, feather, or

bone, tooth, or claw. Its presence serves as an immediate link with the energies it represents. A totem is therefore more effective than a glyph or symbol as an aid to comprehending nonphysical powers and formative forces.

PRIMARY TOTEMS

In Earth Medicine you have three primary totems: a birth totem, a Directional totem, and an Elemental totem. Your *birth totem* is the embodiment of core characteristics that correspond with the dominant aspects of Nature during your birth time.

Symbol of strength

The handle of this Tlingit knife is carved with a raven and a bear head, symbols of insight and inner strength.

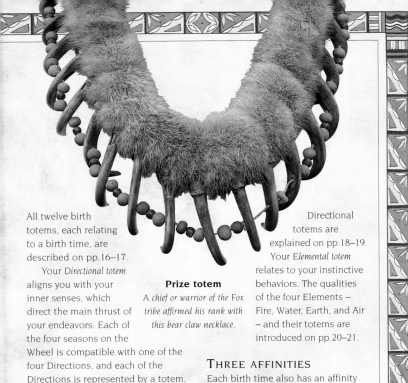

All twelve birth totems, each relating to a birth time, are described on pp. 16–17.

Your *Directional totem* aligns you with your inner senses, which direct the main thrust of your endeavors. Each of the four seasons on the Wheel is compatible with one of the four Directions, and each of the Directions is represented by a totem. For example, Spring is associated with the East, where the sun rises, and signifies seeing things in new ways; its totem is the Eagle. The four

Directional totems are explained on pp. 18–19.

Your *Elemental totem* relates to your instinctive behaviors. The qualities of the four Elements – Fire, Water, Earth, and Air – and their totems are introduced on pp. 20–21.

Prize totem

A chief or warrior of the Fox tribe affirmed his rank with this bear claw necklace.

THREE AFFINITIES

Each birth time also has an affinity with a tree, a stone, and a color (see pp. 36–41). These three affinities have qualities that can strengthen you during challenging times.

"If a man is to succeed, he must be governed not by his inclination, but by an understanding of the ways of animals..." Teton Sioux teaching

15

THE TWELVE
BIRTH TOTEMS

THE TWELVE BIRTH TIMES ARE REPRESENTED BY TOTEMS,
EACH ONE AN ANIMAL THAT BEST EXPRESSES THE
QUALITIES INHERENT IN THAT BIRTH TIME.

E arth Medicine associates an animal totem with each birth time (the two sets of dates below reflect the difference in season between the Northern and Southern Hemispheres). These animals help to connect you to the powers and abilities that they represent. For an in-depth study of the Woodpecker birth totem, see pp.28–29.

FALCON
March 21–April 19 (N. Hem)
Sept 22–Oct 22 (S. Hem)
Falcons are full of initiative, but often rush in to make decisions they may later regret. Lively and extroverted, they have enthusiasm for new experiences but can sometimes lack persistence.

DEER
May 21–June 20 (N. Hem)
Nov 23–Dec 21 (S. Hem)
Deer are willing to sacrifice the old for the new. They loathe routine, thriving on variety and challenges. They have a wild side, often leaping from one situation or relationship into another without reflection.

BEAVER
April 20–May 20 (N. Hem)
Oct 23–Nov 22 (S. Hem)
Practical and steady, Beavers have a capacity for perseverance. Good homemakers, they are warm and affectionate but need harmony and peace to avoid becoming irritable. They have a keen aesthetic sense.

WOODPECKER
June 21–July 21 (N. Hem)
Dec 22–Jan 19 (S. Hem)
Emotional and sensitive, Woodpeckers are warm to those closest to them, and willing to sacrifice their needs for those of their loved ones. They have lively imaginations but can be worriers.

SALMON
July 22 – August 21 (N. Hem)
Jan 20 – Feb 18 (S. Hem)

Enthusiastic and self-confident,
Salmon people enjoy running things.
They are uncompromising and
forceful, and can occasionally seem a
little arrogant or self-important. They
are easily hurt by neglect.

OWL
Nov 23 – Dec 21 (N. Hem)
May 21 – June 20 (S. Hem)

Owls need freedom of expression.
They are lively, self-reliant, and have
an eye for detail. Inquisitive and
adaptable, they have a tendency to
overextend themselves. Owls are
often physically courageous.

BROWN BEAR
August 22 – Sept 21 (N. Hem)
Feb 19 – March 20 (S. Hem)

Brown Bears are hardworking,
practical, and self-reliant. They do
not like change, preferring to stick
to what is familiar. They have a flair
for fixing things, are good-natured,
and make good friends.

GOOSE
Dec 22 – Jan 19 (N. Hem)
June 21 – July 21 (S. Hem)

Goose people are far-sighted
idealists who are willing to explore
the unknown. They approach life with
enthusiasm, determined to fulfill their
dreams. They are perfectionists, and
can appear unduly serious.

CROW
Sept 22 – Oct 22 (N. Hem)
March 21 – April 19 (S. Hem)

Crows dislike solitude and feel most
comfortable in company. Although
usually pleasant and good-natured,
they can be strongly influenced by
negative atmospheres, becoming
gloomy and prickly.

OTTER
Jan 20 – Feb 18 (N. Hem)
July 22 – August 21 (S. Hem)

Otters are friendly, lively, and
perceptive. They feel inhibited by
too many rules and regulations,
which often makes them appear
eccentric. They like cleanliness and
order, and have original minds.

SNAKE
Oct 23 – Nov 22 (N. Hem)
April 20 – May 20 (S. Hem)

Snakes are secretive and
mysterious, hiding their feelings
beneath a cool exterior. Adaptable,
determined, and imaginative, they
are capable of bouncing back from
tough situations encountered in life.

WOLF
Feb 19 – March 20 (N. Hem)
August 22 – Sept 21 (S. Hem)

Wolves are sensitive, artistic, and
intuitive – people to whom others
turn for help. They value freedom
and their own space, and are easily
affected by others. They are
philosophical, trusting, and genuine.

THE INFLUENCE OF THE
DIRECTIONS

ALSO KNOWN BY NATIVE AMERICANS AS THE FOUR
WINDS, THE INFLUENCE OF THE FOUR DIRECTIONS IS
EXPERIENCED THROUGH YOUR INNER SENSES.

Regarded as the "keepers" or "caretakers" of the Universe, the four Directions or alignments were also referred to by Native Americans as the four Winds because their presence was felt rather than seen.

DIRECTIONAL TOTEMS
In Earth Medicine, each Direction or Wind is associated with a season and a time of day. Thus the Summer birth times – Long Days time, Ripening time, and Harvesting time – all

fall within the South Direction, and afternoon. The Direction to which your birth time belongs influences the nature of your inner senses.

The East Direction is associated with illumination. Its totem is the Eagle – a bird that soars closest to the Sun and can see clearly from height. The South is the Direction of Summer and the afternoon. It signifies growth and fruition, fluidity, and emotions. Its totem, the Mouse, symbolizes productivity, feelings, and an ability to perceive detail.

"Remember...the circle of the sky, the stars, the super- natural Winds breathing night and day...the four Directions." Pawnee teaching

The four Directions

Each Direction is associated with a season and a time of day, and also with a principal function: the East with determining, the South with giving, the West with holding, and the North with receiving.

SPRING EQUINOX

NORTH ◄

EAST ◄

BUFFALO

EAGLE

WINTER SOLSTICE

SUMMER SOLSTICE

GRIZZLY BEAR

MOUSE

◄ WEST

SOUTH ◄

AUTUMN EQUINOX

The West is the Direction of Autumn and the evening. It signifies transformation – from day to night, from Summer to Winter – and the qualities of introspection and conservation. Its totem is the Grizzly Bear, which represents strength drawn from within. The North is the Direction of Winter and the night, and is associated with the mind and its sustenance – knowledge. Its totem is the Buffalo, an animal that was honored by Native Americans as the great material "provider."

THE INFLUENCE OF THE ELEMENTS

THE FOUR ELEMENTS – AIR, FIRE, WATER, AND EARTH –
PERVADE EVERYTHING AND INDICATE THE NATURE OF
MOVEMENT AND THE ESSENCE OF WHO YOU ARE.

Elements are intangible qualities that describe the essential state or character of all things. In Earth Medicine, the four Elements are allied with four fundamental modes of activity and are associated with different aspects of the self. Air expresses free movement in all directions; it is related to the mind and to thinking. Fire indicates expansive motion; it is linked with the spirit and with intuition. Water signifies fluidity; it

Elemental profile
*The configuration of
Woodpecker is Water of
Water. Water is both the
Principal Element and
the Elemental Aspect.*

EARTH

FIRE

WATER

WATER

AIR

FIRE

has associations with the soul and the emotions. Earth symbolizes stability; it is related to the physical body and the sensations.

ELEMENTAL DISTRIBUTION

On the Medicine Wheel one Element is associated with each of the four Directions – Fire in the East, Earth in the West, Air in the North, and Water in the South. These are known as the Principal Elements.

The four Elements also have an individual association with each of the twelve birth times – known as the Elemental Aspects. They follow a cyclical sequence around the Wheel based on the action of the Sun (Fire) on the Earth, producing atmosphere (Air) and condensation (Water).

The three birth times that share an Elemental Aspect belong to the same Elemental family or "clan," with a totem that gives insight into its key qualities. Woodpecker people belong to the Frog clan (see pp.34–35).

ELEMENTAL EMPHASIS

For each birth time, the qualities of the Elemental Aspect usually predominate over those of the Principal Element, although both are present to give a specific configuration, such as Fire of Earth (for Woodpecker's, see pp.34–35). For Falcon, Woodpecker, and Otter, the Principal Element and the Elemental Aspect are identical (for example, Air of Air), so people of these totems tend to express that Element intensely.

AIR

WATER

FIRE

EARTH

EARTH

AIR

THE INFLUENCE OF THE MOON

THE WAXING AND WANING OF THE MOON DURING ITS
FOUR PHASES HAS A CRUCIAL INFLUENCE ON THE
FORMATION OF PERSONALITY AND HUMAN ENDEAVOR.

Native Americans regarded the Sun and Moon as indicators respectively of the active and receptive energies inherent in Nature (see p.24), as well as the measurers of time. They associated solar influences with conscious activity and the exercise of reason and the will, and lunar influences with subconscious activity and the emotional and intuitive aspects of human nature.

The Waxing Moon

This phase lasts for approximately eleven days. It is a time of growth and therefore ideal for developing new ideas and concentrating your efforts into new projects.

The Full Moon

Lasting about three days, this is when lunar power is at its height. It is therefore a good time for completing what was developed during the Waxing Moon.

THE FOUR PHASES

There are four phases in the twenty-nine-day lunar cycle, each one an expression of energy reflecting a particular mode of activity. They can be likened to the phases of growth of a flowering plant through the seasons: the emergence of buds (Waxing Moon), the bursting of flowers (Full Moon), the falling away of flowers (Waning Moon), and the germination of seeds (Dark Moon). The influence of each phase can be felt in two ways: in the formation of personality and in day-to-day life.

The energy expressed by the phase of the Moon at the time of your birth has a strong influence on personality. For instance, someone born during the Dark Moon is likely to be inward-looking, while a person born during the Full Moon may be more expressive. Someone born during a Waxing Moon is likely to have an outgoing nature, while a person born during a Waning Moon may be reserved. Consult a set of Moon tables to discover the phase the Moon was in on your birthday.

In your day-to-day life, the benefits of coming into harmony with the Moon's energies are considerable. Experience the energy of the four phases by consciously working with them. A Native American approach is described below.

The Waning Moon

A time for making changes, this phase lasts for an average of eleven days. Use it to improve and modify, and to dispose of what is no longer needed or wanted.

The Dark Moon

The Moon disappears from the sky for around four days. This is a time for contemplation of what has been achieved, and for germinating the seeds for the new.

THE INFLUENCE OF
ENERGY FLOW

THE MEDICINE WHEEL REFLECTS THE PERFECT BALANCE OF THE COMPLEMENTARY ACTIVE AND RECEPTIVE ENERGIES THAT COEXIST IN NATURE.

Energy flows through Nature in two complementary ways, which can be expressed in terms of active and receptive, or male and female. The active energy principle is linked with the Elements of Fire and Air, and the receptive principle with Water and Earth.

Each of the twelve birth times has an active or receptive energy related to its Elemental Aspect. Traveling around the Wheel, the two energies alternate with each birth time, resulting in an equal balance of active and receptive energies, as in Nature.

Active energy is associated with the Sun and conscious activity. Those whose birth times take this principle prefer to pursue experience. They are conceptual,

energetic, outgoing, practical, and analytical. Receptive energy is associated with the Moon and subconscious activity. Those whose birth times take this principle prefer to attract experience. They are intuitive, reflective, conserving, emotional, and nurturing.

THE WAKAN-TANKA

At the heart of the Wheel lies an S-shape within a circle, the symbol of the life-giving source of everything that comes into physical existence – seemingly out of nothing. Named by the Plains Indians as Wakan-Tanka (Great Power), it can also be perceived as energy coming into form and form reverting to energy in the unending continuity of life.

WOODPECKER
MEDICINE

YOUR IN-DEPTH
PERSONALITY PROFILE

SEASON OF BIRTH
LONG DAYS TIME

THE COMFORTING WARMTH OF SUMMER CAN BE FELT
DURING THE FIRST BIRTH TIME OF THE SEASON, LENDING
THOSE BORN THEN THE ABILITY TO NURTURE.

Long Days time is one of the twelve birth times, the fundamental division of the year into twelve seasonal segments (see pp.12–13). As the first period of the Summer cycle, which begins with the Summer solstice, it is a time when solar energies reach their peak and Nature slows its pace after Spring and begins to luxuriate in its abundance.

INFLUENCE OF NATURE

The qualities and characteristics imbued in Nature at this time form the basis of your own nature. So, just as the delicate, fragrant flowers and lush grasses flourish during the long hours of daylight, if you were born during Long Days time you will have a warm and affectionate nature that draws others to you and wins their trust. The mildness of the season matches the placid gentleness of your temperament, which others find comforting, and which enables you to achieve harmony in your relationships. However, like a sultry summer's day, your desire to nurture and protect all those that you value may sometimes prove stifling to them.

Traditionally, the Hopi people began the ceremony of Niman five days after the Summer solstice. The solemn rituals were held to ensure enough rain for a successful harvest, and took place over sixteen days. In the same way, you invest time and care into nurturing your own talents, which should ensure that you reap the benefits during your life.

STAGE OF LIFE

This time of year might be compared to the period of life when youth reaches adulthood. It is a time when the potential of youth is tested and developed through experience. In human development terms, it is the age when you accept your duties and responsibilities, and with them the expectation of harvesting the fruits of your endeavors.

ACHIEVE YOUR POTENTIAL

You enjoy nurturing the talents of others and trust that they will achieve their full potential. You provide a warm, comforting environment for those you care for, enabling them to develop at their own pace to full

Nature's energy

The nurturing power of Nature comes into play in this, the first cycle of Summer after the Summer solstice. The intoxicating fragrance of flowers fills the air and the ground is covered with lush vegetation.

maturity. You become attached, even devoted, to the people and things you are helping to develop. However, you can become resentful and bitter if a project close to your heart is canceled, or someone to whom you are devoted suddenly turns against you.

Beware of investing so much of your emotional energy into a project or person that you cannot bear to withdraw or let go. Try also not to become overprotective of your family and close friends.

"Life is a circle from childhood to childhood; so it is with everything where power moves." Black Elk teaching

BIRTH TOTEM
THE WOODPECKER

THE ESSENTIAL NATURE AND CHARACTERISTIC BEHAVIOR
OF THE WOODPECKER EXPRESSES THE PERSONALITY TYPE
OF THOSE BORN DURING LONG DAYS TIME.

L ike the woodpecker, people born during Long Days time are nurturing, protective, and tenacious. If you were born at this time, you have a warm, emotional, sensitive nature that leads you to develop strong attachments to people and projects.

Home is important to you, and you enjoy creating an attractive, comfortable environment for yourself and your family. Your devotion to your family can sometimes mean that you are over-protective of your children, reluctant to allow them to leave the nest when they are ready to go.

Kind and considerate, you are easily upset by insensitive behavior. You tend to allow your heart to rule your head, sometimes resulting in rash judgments, which you later regret.

A strong commitment to your beliefs and friends makes you a loyal friend and employee. Indeed, you sometimes sacrifice your own needs in your desire to serve others, resulting in bitter self-recrimination.

HEALTH MATTERS

You have a tendency to put your lively imagination and turbulent emotions to unproductive use by worrying unduly about your future security. The anxiety you cause yourself in this way usually manifests itself physically in a stomach disorder, for your stomach is your most vulnerable area. Although robust and quick to recover from most illnesses, you tend to have a low pain threshold and can be rather demanding when unwell.

Woodpecker power

Protective, colorful, and tenacious, the woodpecker also expresses the intense, sensitive aspects of the emotional and caring people born at this time.

THE WOODPECKER AND
RELATIONSHIPS

CONSIDERATE AND SENSITIVE, WOODPECKER PEOPLE ARE
LOYAL AND VALUED FRIENDS. THEY CAN MAKE DEVOTED
PARTNERS BUT TEND TO BE OVERPROTECTIVE.

Emotional and nurturing, Woodpecker people, like their totem animal, cling tenaciously to what they hold dear. If your birth totem is Woodpecker, you form strong attachments and enjoy close friendships but may become overattached. You tend to be less at ease with acquaintances and strangers, with whom you may appear cool and even unfriendly.

LOVING RELATIONSHIPS

Woodpeckers thrive on total commitment and need a close relationship in order to feel secure. Male Woodpeckers are protective and patient, while female Woodpeckers are very caring and can be sexually assertive. Both are sensitive but may be overemotional, and are easily hurt or disappointed.

When problems arise, it is generally because of your inability to let go – you can seem smothering. At times, you can be snappy and moody or preoccupied with your own woes, in sharp contrast to your otherwise kind and understanding nature.

COPING WITH WOODPECKER

Woodpecker people are extremely emotional and sensitive creatures and should be handled gently. Protective of others, they are highly vulnerable themselves and will soon withdraw if they feel threatened, appearing bitter and defensive. Be positive in their company; their sensitivity means that they are easily influenced by others' moods. They are natural worriers, so offering frequent reassurance helps them to relax and be less clingy.

WOODPECKER IN LOVE

Woodpecker with Falcon
Both want security, but Falcon's impetuous nature may not suit Woodpecker's desire for tenderness.

Woodpecker with Beaver
Both require a settled and comfortable home. Beaver adds sound common sense to Woodpecker's sensitivity.

Woodpecker with Deer
This can be a lively match if Woodpecker can overcome Deer's impetuosity.

Woodpecker with Woodpecker Both crave affection and support each other's sensitivity. Problems arise if they have emotional upheavals at the same time.

Woodpecker with Salmon
Woodpecker enjoys Salmon's caring nature but may find Salmon too demanding.

Woodpecker with Brown Bear Warm and affectionate Woodpecker can form a contented relationship with considerate Brown Bear.

Woodpecker with Crow
Both are romantics, but Crow must find a way to handle Woodpecker's possessive emotions.

Woodpecker with Snake
This can be a highly charged partnership, for the intensity of each can divide them or create a deeper bond.

Woodpecker with Owl
Woodpecker wants to nurture and protect while Owl likes to be free, so this can lead to conflict.

Woodpecker with Goose
Both have traditional values, but Goose tends to put practicalities before romance.

Woodpecker with Otter
Woodpecker may find Otter's unconventionality unsettling, while Otter may rebel to avoid being smothered.

Woodpecker with Wolf
Nurturing Woodpecker and compassionate Wolf should be a good match. Each can clear up differences quickly.

DIRECTIONAL TOTEM
THE MOUSE

THE MOUSE SYMBOLIZES THE INFLUENCE OF THE SOUTH
ON WOODPECKER PEOPLE, WHO USE THEIR SENSITIVITY
AND EMOTIONS TO POWER THEIR UNDERSTANDING.

Long Days time, Ripening time, and Harvesting time all fall within the quarter of the Medicine Wheel associated with the South Direction or Wind. The South is aligned with Summer and the bright warmth of midday, and it is associated with trust and innocence, depth of feeling, a sense of wonder, and hope. The power of the South's influence is primarily with the emotions, and its principal function is the power of giving. It takes as its totem the sensitive, curious, easily overlooked mouse.

The specific influence of the South on Woodpecker people is on feelings and trusting your instincts. The South Wind in this period

Warrior Mouse doll
This Hopi Kachina doll represents the mouse, which is associated with emotional sensitivity.

imparts an easy understanding of your own heart felt emotions, enabling you to love unselfishly. The South was sometimes known as "the way of the child" because it was associated with trust in the true self and the avoidance of cynicism or arrogance.

MOUSE CHARACTERISTICS
The mouse has whiskers that make it particularly sensitive to its surroundings, so Native Americans believed it symbolized the power of

perception through closeness and through feelings. Its tiny size means it may be disregarded – just as we often overlook the small, true voice of our inner self. It also expresses curiosity, the value of experiencing through exploration and involvement, and a capacity to learn and develop at considerable speed.

The spirit of the South

The Sun is at its zenith in the South, symbolizing joy in life; the Mouse totem signifies heightened perception.

If your Directional totem is Mouse, you are likely to be highly sensitive to atmosphere and to the moods of those around you. Your actions and decisions are often influenced by your emotions, which you need to balance with your inner wisdom. You pay close attention to detail, have the ability to learn and make rapid development, and know that great achievements may grow from small beginnings.

ELEMENTAL TOTEM
THE FROG

LIKE THE FROG, WHICH FEELS EVERY RIPPLE IN THE WATER, WOODPECKER PEOPLE'S HIGHLY SENSITIVE NATURE REQUIRES FREE EXPRESSION.

The Elemental Aspect of Woodpecker people is Water. They share this Aspect with Snake and Wolf people, who all therefore belong to the same Elemental family or "clan" (see pp. 20–21 for an introduction to the influence of the Elements). Each Elemental clan has a totem to provide insight into its essential characteristics.

THE FROG CLAN

The totem of the Elemental clan of Water is Frog, which symbolizes a sensitive, emotional, thoughtful, and intuitive nature.

The frog is at home both in water and on land, diving below the surface then sitting still, attuned to every movement around it. So, if you belong to this clan you have the ability to adapt, while your intuition enables you to see beneath surface

Below the surface
The frog symbolizes the fundamental quality of Water: deep sensitivity.

appearances and to understand the moods of others.

Imaginative, responsive, and intense, you have deep emotions, which you "bottle up" at times. You dislike feeling vulnerable and can be secretive. You crave understanding and true freedom to express yourself both creatively and emotionally.

Water of Water

The Element of Water feeds Water, generating deeply felt emotions and intuition.

When you are faced with problems arising from these situations, you can become negative, bitter, and unhappy. At times like these, or when you are stressed or are facing a dilemma, try the following revitalizing exercise.

ELEMENTAL PROFILE

For Woodpecker people, the predominant Elemental Aspect of emotional Water is pure and undiluted because your Principal Element is also Water. If you were born at this time, you are likely to feel emotions very deeply and have an intuitive understanding of the feelings of others.

You may have a tendency to be oversensitive and to let your emotions run you, driven by the turbulent power of Water. So you may sometimes find yourself feeling upset and out of control.

You have a natural affinity with water, and it can soothe you, so find a quiet spot by a river or lake, by the sea, or even by a pool or fountain, away from the polluting effects of traffic and the activities of others.

Enjoy the play of light or reflections on the surface, and let the sound of the water wash over you as you breathe slowly and deeply. With each in-breath, acknowledge that you are absorbing the energizing power of the life force. Feel it course through your body, bringing you the clarity of a mountain stream, and refreshing body, mind, and spirit.

STONE AFFINITY
ROSE QUARTZ

By using the gemstone with which your own essence resonates, you can tap into the power of the Earth itself and awaken your inner strengths.

Faceted rose quartz
Rose quartz is a gemstone that is believed to heal emotional hurts and strengthen bonds of kinship.

Gemstones are minerals that are formed within the Earth itself in an exceedingly slow but continuous process. Native Americans valued gemstones not only for their beauty but also for being literally part of the Earth, and therefore possessing part of its life force. They regarded gemstones as being "alive" – channelers of energy that could be used in many ways: to heal, to protect, or for meditation.

Every gemstone has a different energy or vibration. On the Medicine Wheel, a stone is associated with each birth time, the energy of which resonates with the essence of those born during that time. Because of this energy affiliation, your stone can be used to help bring you into harmony with the Earth and to create balance within yourself. It can enhance and develop your good qualities and endow you with the abilities you need.

ENERGY RESONANCE

Woodpecker people have an affinity with rose quartz – a type of quartz with a delicate pink color, thought to be due to traces of titanium. Sometimes known as the "love stone," rose quartz is thought to soothe the emotions and bring

ACTIVATE YOUR GEMSTONE

Obtain a piece of rose quartz and cleanse it by holding it under cold running water. Allow it to dry naturally. Then, holding the stone with both hands, bring it up to your mouth and blow into it sharply and hard, three or four times in order to impregnate it with your breath. Next, hold it firmly in one hand, and silently welcome it into your life as a friend and helper.

When faced with a sudden problem, use the rose quartz to help you meditate. Find a quiet spot to lie down, and place the rose quartz on your breastbone. Close your eyes and visualize its warm, pink light entering you, bringing you a solution. Listen for the still, small voice of your inner self.

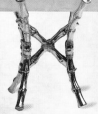

tenderness to relationships. Considered by Native Americans as helpful in healing emotional wounds and restoring self-esteem, it is said to calm the mind, particularly after a turbulent experience. This gemstone is also thought to promote receptivity to beauty of all kinds.

If your birth totem is Woodpecker, you will find rose quartz especially helpful when you are faced with

Rose quartz power
To benefit most from its effect, keep a piece of rose quartz with you at all times, and place some in key positions in your home to help create a peaceful atmosphere.

sudden difficulties. Its gentle, calming energy enhances your insight, making it a valuable aid in times of crisis or during emotional or troubled situations.

"The outline of the stone is round; the power of the stone is endless." Lakota Sioux teaching

TREE AFFINITY
ASPEN

GAIN A DEEPER UNDERSTANDING OF YOUR OWN NATURE
AND AWAKEN POWERS LYING DORMANT WITHIN YOU BY
RESPECTING AND CONNECTING WITH YOUR AFFINITY TREE.

Trees have an important part to play in the protection of Nature's mechanisms and in the maintenance of the Earth's atmospheric balance, which is essential for the survival of the human race.

Native Americans referred to trees as "Standing People" because they stand firm, obtaining strength from their connection with the Earth. They therefore teach us the importance of being grounded, while at the same time listening to and reaching for our higher

aspirations. When respected as living beings, trees can provide insight into the workings of Nature and our own inner selves.

On the Medicine Wheel, each birth time is associated with a particular kind of tree, the basic qualities of which complement the nature of those born during that time. Woodpecker people have an affinity with the aspen. A vigorous tree, it carries its strength with grace, and its characteristic whispering leaves suggest that Woodpecker people can also express their strong

CONNECT WITH YOUR TREE

Appreciate the beauty of your affinity tree and study its nature carefully, for it has an affinity with your own nature.

The aspen is a type of poplar. It is a vigorous yet graceful tree, with small leaves that quiver in the slightest breeze, so it is sometimes known as the "trembling tree." This rustling of its leaves creates a gentle whispering sound.

Try the following exercise when you need to revitalize your inner strength. Stand beside your affinity tree. Place the palms of your hands on its trunk and rest your forehead on the backs of your hands. Inhale slowly and let energy from the tree's roots flow through your body. If easily available, obtain a cutting or twig from your affinity tree to keep as a totem or helper.

feelings with gentleness. The aspen's trembling echoes Woodpecker's deep sensitivity, or oversensitivity at times. In emotionally charged situations, Woodpecker people can tap into their own powers of quiet strength and restraint by connecting with their tree (see panel above).

OVERCOMING FEARS

If your birth totem is Woodpecker, you have a nurturing and emotional nature. The adverse side of such sensitivity is a tendency to worry, which can make you overcautious and moody, or lead to stagnation.

However, just as wood from the aspen was used for shields to bolster defenses, you can also strengthen your resolve and find hope and resilience in the face of risk and uncertainty. Draw on the power of the aspen to provide you with the vigor and energy that will enable you to calm your fears and follow the path your heart tells you is right.

"All healing plants are given by Wakan-Tanka; therefore they are holy." **Lakota Sioux teaching**

COLOR AFFINITY
ROSE

Enhance your positive qualities by using the power of your affinity color to affect your emotional and mental states.

Each birth time has an affinity with a particular color. This is the color that resonates best with the energies of the people born during that time. Exposure to your affinity color will encourage a positive emotional and mental response, while exposure to colors that clash with your affinity color will have a negative effect on your sense of well-being.

The color rose resonates with Woodpecker people. Made up of equal parts red and white, rose combines the influence of both these colors. Red is associated with vibrant passionate energy and white with peace and tranquillity; mixed together as rose, they embody strong caring and protectiveness. Essentially a soothing color, rose can ease negative feelings and anger, and help you deal more effectively with stress.

In addition to its kind, gentle associations, rose also stimulates energy levels and emotional tenacity. It is the

Color scheme

Let a rose color theme be the thread that runs through your entire home, from the ornaments to the walls and floors.

BATHE IN YOUR COLOR

Take a bottle of rose aroma-therapy oil and add a few drops to your bath water. Gently stir the water to disperse the oil before climbing in. When you are ready, submerge your body in the water. Make sure you have at least half an hour to spare so you can indulge in a relaxed, unhurried soaking.

Relaxing in a rose-oil bath will release tension, relieve stress, and leave your skin feeling soft and smooth. It is especially beneficial if you are feeling emotionally drained, depressed, or are suffering from low self-esteem. Allow any thoughts and sensations to flow through your mind and body, and reflect on them.

color of vitality blended with altruism and calm discrimination to embody an affectionate, nurturing emotional energy that is constant and sensitive rather than volatile or intensely passionate.

COLOR BENEFITS

Strengthen your aura and enhance your positive qualities by introducing shades of rose – soft pink and pale crimson – to the interior decor of your home. Spots of color can make

all the difference. For example, a rose-tinted lampshade can alter the ambience of a room, or try displaying a vase of roses – a traditional token of love and affection – in a pale pink vase.

If you need a confidence boost, wear something that contains rose. Whenever your energies are low, practice the color bathing exercise outlined above to balance your emotions, awaken your creativity, and help you to feel joyful.

"The power of the spirit should be honored with its color." *Lakota Sioux teaching*

WORKING THE WHEEL
LIFE PATH

CONSIDER YOUR BIRTH PROFILE AS A STARTING POINT IN
THE DEVELOPMENT OF YOUR CHARACTER AND THE
ACHIEVEMENT OF PERSONAL FULFILLMENT.

Each of the twelve birth times is associated with a particular path of learning or with a collection of lessons to be learned through life. By following your path of learning, you will develop strengths in place of weaknesses, achieve a greater sense of harmony with the world, and discover inner peace.

YOUR PATH OF LEARNING
For Woodpecker people, the first lesson on your path of learning is to overcome your

tendency to spend much of your time worrying about events that may never happen or situations in the past that you might have handled differently. You imagine the end of a relationship when it has only just begun and mull over the different path your career might have taken had you behaved differently at a certain point. Let go of regrets concerning the past and banish

"Each man's road is shown to him within his own heart. There he sees all the truths of life." Cheyenne teaching

42

doubts about the future. Instead, live in the present and experience fully what is happening now. In this way, you will lead a more enjoyable and fulfilling life.

Woodpecker people also need to learn how to control their turbulent emotions and possessiveness. Deeply loving and sensitive, you are easily hurt, which can lead to irrational outbursts and bitter recriminations. Remember, those close to you usually do not mean to be hurtful, so try to put their behavior in perspective and allow them the space they need.

Your third lesson is to recognize that life's trials, conflicts, successes, and failures are all valuable experiences in your personal development. Do not allow setbacks in love or work to demotivate you or make you miserable. Try to remain positive and regard any disappointments as challenges in your path to becoming a stronger, more fulfilled person.

MEDICINE POWER

HARNESS THE POWERS OF OTHER BIRTH TIMES TO TRANSFORM YOUR WEAKNESSES INTO STRENGTHS AND TO MEET THE CHALLENGES IN YOUR LIFE.

The whole spectrum of human qualities and abilities is represented on the Medicine Wheel. The totems and affinities associated with each birth time indicate the basic qualities with which those born at that time are equipped.

Study your path of learning (see pp.42–43) to identify those aspects of your personality that may need to be strengthened, then look at other birth times to discover the totems and affinities that can assist you in this task. For example, your Elemental profile is Water of Water (see pp.34–35), so for balance you need the stabilizing qualities of

Complementary affinity

A key strength of Goose – weak in Woodpecker – is the ability to be objective.

Earth, the freedom of Air, and the enthusiasm of Fire. Otter's Elemental profile is Air of Air, Beaver's is Earth of Fire, and Owl's is Fire of Earth, so meditate on these birth totems. In addition, you may find it useful to study the profiles of the other two members of your Elemental clan of Frog – Snake and Wolf – to discover how the same Elemental Aspect of Water can be expressed differently.

Also helpful is the birth totem opposite yours on the Wheel, which contains qualities that complement or enhance your own. This is known as your complementary affinity, which for Woodpecker people is Goose.

ESSENTIAL STRENGTHS

Described below are the essential strengths of each birth totem. To develop a quality that is weak in yourself or that you need to meet a particular challenge, meditate upon the birth totem that contains the attribute you need. Obtain a representation of the relevant totem – a claw, tooth, or feather; a picture, ring, or model. Affirm that the power it represents is within you.

Falcon medicine is the power of keen observation and the ability to act decisively and energetically whenever action is required..

Beaver medicine is the ability to think creatively and laterally – to develop alternative ways of doing or thinking about things.

Deer medicine is characterized by sensitivity to the intentions of others and to that which might be detrimental to your well-being.

Woodpecker medicine is the ability to establish a steady rhythm throughout life and to be tenacious in protecting all that you value.

Salmon medicine is the strength to be determined and courageous in the choice of goals you want to achieve and to have enough stamina to see a task through to the end.

Brown Bear medicine is the ability to be resourceful, hardworking, and dependable in times of need, and to draw on inner strength.

Crow medicine is the ability to transform negative or nonproductive situations into positive ones and to transcend limitations.

Snake medicine is the talent to adapt easily to changes in circumstances and to manage transitional phases well.

Owl medicine is the power to see clearly during times of uncertainty and to conduct life consistently, according to long-term plans.

Goose medicine is the courage to do whatever might be necessary to protect your ideals and to adhere to your principles in life.

Otter medicine is the ability to connect with your inner child, to be innovative and idealistic, and to thoroughly enjoy the ordinary tasks and routines of everyday life.

Wolf medicine is the courage to act according to your intuition and instincts rather than your intellect, and to be compassionate.